T0130238

# THREE YEARS AND THREE SUMMERS

## MOMMA GOES AWAY TO COLLEGE

*By*
*Sharon Butts-Pierce*

*Illustrated by Sydnee Lunderman*

AuthorHouse™
1663 Liberty Drive
Bloomington, IN 47403
www.authorhouse.com
Phone: 833-262-8899

Because of the dynamic nature of the Internet, any web addresses or links contained in this book may have changed since publication and may no longer be valid. The views expressed in this work are solely those of the author and do not necessarily reflect the views of the publisher, and the publisher hereby disclaims any responsibility for them.

Any people depicted in stock imagery provided by Getty Images are models, and such images are being used for illustrative purposes only.
Certain stock imagery © Getty Images.

This book is printed on acid-free paper.

ISBN: 978-1-6655-5479-4 (sc)
978-1-6655-5480-0 (e)

Library of Congress Control Number: 2022905026

Print information available on the last page.

Published by AuthorHouse  03/16/2022

author HOUSE®

# About the Author

**Sharon Butts Pierce** was born and raised in Belle Glade, Florida. Sharon went away to Saint Augustine, Florida in 1960 and attended Webster Elementary School while her mother attended college for three years and three summers. Sharon returned home to Belle Glade in 1963 and graduated as Valedictorian of Lake Shore High School Class of 1969. After earning an Associate of Arts Degree from Palm Beach Junior College, Sharon attended University of Florida and is one of 123 black students who withdrew and left the university during the 1971 Sit-In and civil rights protests. Sharon earned a Bachelor of Science Degree, Mathematics Major, from Florida State University in 1972.

Sharon retired in 2000 from BellSouth after serving twenty-seven years as a Telecommunications Manager. She faithfully guided families home for ten years as a licensed Real Estate Salesperson in Georgia and is the Owner of Shallou Butts, LLC. Sharon Butts Pierce was happily married for forty-nine years to Curtis Lee Pierce, a graduate of Florida Memorial College, Retired Professional Educator, Retired U.S. Army SFC and founding Chief Executive Officer of Lake Shore High School Legacy Park Memorial, LLC. Sharon is a proud Blue Star Mother of two U.S. Army Veterans and a Grateful Grandmother of five precious ones.

For Curtis II, Cursha, Aleyna, Sydnee, Isaiah, Ayden and Micah, two grandchildren and five great-grandchildren of Charles Lee Butts, Sr. and Ruby Pearl Keith Butts. You are the pride and joy of generations of honorable men and wise women. God loves you! I love you!

My first grade teacher was the best ever!

Last year my second grade teacher taught me the part of POLLY-MAKE-BELIEVE for my school play.

This year my third grade teacher is smart, gentle and kind. Soon I am going to fourth grade!

# POLLY

# MAKE-BELIEVE

# AN

# OPERETTA

# IN TWO ACTS

# April 30, 1959

# 8:15 P.M.

# Lake Shore Hi Gym

I am happy running home from school and playing in the backyard. I am happy walking to great-grandma Doll's house with my two sisters and one brother. I am happy when Momma cooks dinner and sets the table at night. I am happy when Daddy comes home from work to eat dinner. I am happy when Daddy makes lemonade with me!

At summer end, Daddy says that Momma is going away to college. Going away to college? Where is college? What is college? What will happen to me, my two sisters and one brother?

Daddy says that Momma is going away to college for three years and three summers. All four of you are going too when Momma goes away to college!

College is a school after twelfth grade for boys, girls, men and women. When Momma goes away to college, I am going away with Momma to live in a new city. I am sad to go away to a new school.

COLLEGE
12TH GRADE
11TH GRADE
10TH GRADE
9TH GRADE
8TH GRADE
7TH GRADE
6TH GRADE
5TH GRADE
4TH GRADE
3RD GRADE
2ND GRADE
1ST GRADE

One day we pack our clothes and put bags of food inside Daddy's big car. Daddy says to Momma, to me, to my two sisters and one brother to get ready for a long ride.

Daddy drives us far away to the new house in the new city of Saint Augustine. I give hugs and wave goodbye to Daddy. I am sad. I start fourth grade at the new school on Monday and Momma starts year one of college!

Saint Augustine is the oldest city in Florida. Trees are old and full of moss. I miss Palm trees and coconuts. I miss my friends. I miss great-grandma Doll's house.

My fourth grade teacher is nice. She shows and tells me all about the new school.

On long walks from the new school to the new house my two sisters and one brother and I pick up empty soda bottles from the ground and carry them to the store. We sell the empty soda bottles to the store owner and he gives us pennies to buy cookies!

Momma goes to school five days a week in year one of college. Momma says that going away to college is the key to getting a high paying job to make dreams come true. I love Momma.

Momma keeps her school work in big notebooks!! Momma reads many books in college and she paints beautiful pictures of still fruit.

My two sisters and one brother and I pick real fruit from the blackberry bush behind the new house. After Momma does her homework Momma cooks sweet blackberry doo-bee for dessert.

Today Momma starts year two of college and I start fifth grade. My fifth grade teacher is a gentleman. He looks like Daddy!

Daddy comes once a month to bring money from his paycheck and fresh food from the fields of Belle Glade. Daddy works two jobs. His day job is at the Experiment Station. His night job is at the big pink hospital where I was born. I hope Daddy comes soon and brings fresh food for us to eat on Sunday.

I eat free and reduced lunch at school five days a week! Free and reduced lunch is delicious!

I am happy that I got promoted to sixth grade. My sixth grade teacher is my last teacher in Saint Augustine! This year Momma has many more books to read in year three of college.

Momma says the four of you need to help with chores. On Saturday the four of us sweep floors. We put away clean clothes from the laundromat! We fold beautiful bed quilts made with love by great-grandma Doll.

Daddy comes in his big car on Momma's last day of college! Momma wears a beautiful black dress to her college graduation. Daddy wears a fine suit and tie!

Momma is now a first grade teacher! Momma is now the best first grade teacher ever! I am happy getting inside Daddy's big car for the long ride home to Belle Glade.

# About Mrs. Ruby Pearl Keith Butts

**Ruby Pearl Keith Butts** graduated with a Bachelor of Science Degree, Education Major, with Honors in 1963 from Florida Normal and Industrial Memorial College located in Saint Augustine, Florida. Mrs. Butts and her four children went away from their home in Belle Glade, Florida and lived in Saint Augustine, Florida for three years including summers to complete her College degree program. Her four children attended Webster Elementary School. The College which she attended is an HBCU, was renamed to Florida Memorial College, relocated to Miami, Florida in 1968 and changed its name to Florida Memorial University in 2006.

Mrs. Butts dedicated thirty-five years of service to the education profession instructing students enrolled in Palm Beach County Public Schools including Canal Point Elementary and Gove Elementary. Mrs. Butts poured into thousands of students inspiring them to graduate and to reach incredible career heights including professional football players. Community and Service affiliations were: Member of Mt. Zion African Methodist Episcopal Church, Sigma Gamma Rho Sorority, National Education Association and Florida Retired Educators Association.

# Mrs. Ruby Pearl Keith Butts

**Ruby Pearl Keith** was born in Pahokee, Florida and graduated from Everglades Vocational High School. She was united in marriage to Charles Lee Butts, Sr. for forty-eight years. Charles "Charlie" Butts graduated from Everglades Vocational High School, attended HBCU Florida A&M University on a football scholarship and served as a Director with Everglades Progressive Citizens, Inc.

Printed in the United States
by Baker & Taylor Publisher Services